Original title:

Labyrinth of the Silent Echo

Author: Liisi Lendorav

ISBN HARDBACK: 978-1-80565-115-4

ISBN PAPERBACK: 978-1-80565-318-9

The Untangling of the Quiet Web

In the hush of the twilight air,
Whispers weave a tapestry rare.
Threads of silver, spun with care,
Hold the secrets that we dare.

Glistening in the fading light,
Hidden corners, nestled tight.
The moon reveals the veiled sight,
Of dreams fluttering, taking flight.

Ancient sounds of the night call,
Echoes of magic, soft and small.
A world unfolds beyond the wall,
Where shadows dance and senses enthrall.

Curiosities stir from their beds,
In the silence, where wonder spreads.
Each thread whispers tales unsaid,
Of enchantments laced with dread.

So gather round, dear hearts, and see,
The quiet web's strange mystery.
For in its folds lies a key,
To the magic that sets us free.

Secrets Swirling in the Silent Abyss

Within the deep, where shadows dwell,
Lies a tale the stars could tell.
Echoes of time, a haunting spell,
In murky waters, dreams compel.

Ripples whisper through the gloom,
Tracing lines of hidden doom.
In the silence, secrets bloom,
Songs of sorrow, tales of gloom.

Eyes of night, piercing and wise,
Watch the surface, where truth lies.
Beneath the waves, the heart defies,
As ghosts of past slowly rise.

Captured moments, lost in time,
Notes forgotten, rhyme sublime.
In the abyss, a silent chime,
Resonates with every crime.

So dive below, where fears take flight,
And unravel the threads of night.
For in the depths, there burns a light,
Guiding souls through endless night.

The Silent Symphony of the Mind

In realms where thoughts like whispers weave,
A melody, both bright and naïve.
Hidden notes in shadows play,
A symphony that won't decay.

Between the sighs and fleeting dreams,
Each silence flows like silver streams.
The heart beats soft, a gentle guide,
As secrets in the quiet reside.

Fragments dance in twilight's glow,
In chambers where no footsteps go.
A tapestry of whispered light,
Forgotten visions take their flight.

With every thought, a story's spun,
A world created, never done.
The silent song within the mind,
A harmony both rare and blind.

Unfolding in the Midst of Shadows

In shadows deep where secrets nest,
The world unveils its hidden quest.
Tendrils of dusk caress the ground,
While echoes whisper all around.

The moonbeams brush the ancient trees,
With tales carried on the breeze.
A flickering light, a ghostly trace,
In every fold, a quiet grace.

Veils of night, a shroud of dreams,
Born from the heart of moonlit beams.
Darkness blooms, a fragrant flower,
In silence lies unspoken power.

Footsteps soft like falling leaves,
Reveal the truth that darkness weaves.
In shadows, whispers come alive,
A hidden world where spirits thrive.

The Sigh of Unseen Corners

In corners where the light grows dim,
A sigh escapes on whispers' whim.
Dancing dust in twilight's breath,
A fleeting trace of life and death.

Beneath the stairs, the stories hide,
Of moments lost that still abide.
In echoes soft, the past can drift,
Among the shadows, dreams can lift.

Secrets clung to worn-out chairs,
The silence sings of hidden cares.
In gentle folds of time's embrace,
Unseen corners find their place.

A warmth remains, though light has fled,
In hidden paths where dreams are fed.
The sigh of life, of hope, of fears,
Whispers sweetly through our years.

Wandering Through Echoes of Time

In corridors where echoes play,
The past still calls, a soft ballet.
With every step, a story flows,
A river where the memory grows.

Through ancient halls of whispered grace,
Time weaves its dance, its soft embrace.
Each echo holds a laughter sweet,
A melody of hearts that meet.

Wandering paths of faded light,
We search for dreams that take their flight.
In every heartbeat, time's refrain,
A song of joy, a thread of pain.

In twilight's glow, the past awakes,
As shadows stir and daylight breaks.
The journey's threads connect us all,
In echoes soft, we rise, we fall.

The Soundless Spiral

In shadows deep where secrets dwell,
A spiral winds, a hushed farewell.
Whispers dance on air so light,
In muted tones, they fade from sight.

The stars above spin tales untold,
Of dreams and fears both brave and bold.
Yet silence wraps the secrets tight,
As darkness swallows gifted light.

A flicker here, a shimmer there,
The soundless spiral of despair.
With every turn, enchantments weave,
A tapestry that none perceive.

In corners where the lost ones glide,
The haunting echoes cannot hide.
With each soft sigh, the night will sigh,
In whispered tones, like lullabies.

Trails of the Unsung

Beneath the weight of stars unknown,
The trails of unsung softly moan.
A memory that time forgot,
In every heart, a sacred spot.

Through dusty paths, the lost ones tread,
In silence loud as words unsaid.
Each step a story, lightly penned,
In pages worn, where shadows blend.

The whispers of a gentle past,
In echoes linger, unsurpassed.
They guide the souls still yet to roam,
To find in silence, their true home.

For every heart that beats alone,
On trails of the unsung is sown.
A flicker of light in endless night,
To lead them forth through dark to bright.

Mirrors in the Hushed Corners

In corners hushed where shadows play,
The mirrors gleam, a ghostly ray.
Reflecting dreams of souls once near,
And laughter lost, now laced with fear.

Amidst the stillness, secrets glow,
In frames of silver, tales bestow.
Each glance held tight, a fleeting dance,
In whispered worlds of happenstance.

With every ripple, time unfolds,
The echoes of the brave and bold.
They linger there in silent grace,
In mirrors' arms, a soft embrace.

So journey forth through muted halls,
Where silence softly beckons all.
In hushed corners, life shall weave,
A tapestry that won't deceive.

The Riddle of Echoing Footsteps

In moonlit nights, the echoes tread,
With whispers soft as words unsaid.
Footsteps dance down forgotten ways,
In riddles wrapped, the night conveys.

Each step a tale of yore and pause,
In shadows deep, where silence draws.
The riddles float on midnight air,
Entwined with dreams, a silent snare.

They beckon forth the brave and wise,
To follow paths 'neath starry skies.
A journey bound by questions bold,
In tales of time and love retold.

So listen close, heed every sound,
In echo's realm, the lost are found.
For wisdom's song in footsteps dwell,
A riddle wrapped in magic's spell.

Silenced Strings of the Mind

In twilight's grasp, the thoughts do weave,
A tapestry of hopes, that few believe.
Each string, a memory, tugged with care,
Yet silence reigns, an echoing lair.

Whispers float on the breeze of night,
Shadows dance beneath pale moonlight.
The heart, a drum, beats soft and low,
While dreams take flight, then quickly go.

A phantom tune, so sweet, so clear,
Plays softly, yet sounds disappear.
Each note a tale, untold, unseen,
Lost in the depths where shadows glean.

In the stillness, secrets roam,
Searching for a place called home.
With every breath, a symphony sighs,
In the silence, the spirit flies.

So listen close to the muted sound,
Within the mind where hope is found.
For even in silence, stories bloom,
In the quiet, we find our room.

The Hushed Odyssey of the Soul

Across the stars, a journey unfolds,
In whispered dreams, the heart beholds.
Each step echoes a path unknown,
Through realms where only shadows roam.

The soul, a breeze, silently drifts,
Carried by fate, through time it shifts.
A tapestry woven with threads of light,
Guides the wanderer into the night.

In tranquil lakes, reflections gleam,
Each drop a fragment of a dream.
Ripples dance in the endless blue,
As the hushed odyssey bids adieu.

With every sigh, the heart takes flight,
Boundless journeys in realms of night.
A silent oath, in shadows sworn,
To find the dawn, where hope is born.

So venture forth, dear traveler bold,
Seek the stories yet untold.
For within the silence, the truths await,
In hushed whispers, they cherish fate.

Resonance of the Unheard Whisper

A whisper stirs in the depths of thought,
Such soft echoes of lessons taught.
Through stillness, it finds a timeless grace,
An unheard song in a secret place.

Each gentle breath, a tale retold,
In quiet corners, where memories unfold.
The resonance lingers, a subtle tone,
Connecting the heart to the unknown.

With every heartbeat, the echoes swell,
A symphony lost, a magic spell.
In shadows they rise, unseen yet felt,
The warmth of whispers, perfectly dealt.

In solitude's arms, the soul takes flight,
Drifting softly into the night.
A chorus of dreams, too faint to hear,
Yet guiding the heart, ever near.

So heed the silence, embrace the sound,
In each quiet moment, life's treasures abound.
For within the whispers, the truest art,
Resides in the echoes of the heart.

The Echoing Silence of Forgotten Dreams

In the corners of the mind, dreams retreat,
Fading softly, bittersweet.
Once vibrant hues now turned to gray,
The echoing silence leads them astray.

A flutter of wings, a sigh of hope,
Through tangled paths, we learn to cope.
Each slumbering thought, a tale unsung,
While the heart hums tunes it once had strung.

In the quiet hours, shadows play,
Chasing glimpses of the light of day.
The whisper of wishes, a dim refrain,
In the silence, they yearn again.

Yet softly they linger, like morning dew,
Reminding us of what we once knew.
In the echoing silence, we find the key,
Unlocking the door to what was meant to be.

So cherish the stillness, embrace the dream,
For in its depths, our spirits gleam.
In the echoing silence, we learn to see,
The beauty of what was, and still could be.

The Still Voice of the Hidden Night

In shadows deep where secrets dwell,
A whispered breeze, a soft farewell.
The stars align, their stories told,
In silent night, the dreams unfold.

With every sigh, the moonlight glows,
A guardian through the night that flows.
It watches close, a silent guide,
As we traverse the worlds inside.

Each rustling leaf, a tale begun,
Of hidden realms where spirits run.
Beneath the sky, a cloak of grace,
Embraced by night, we find our place.

In corners dark, where shadows play,
The still voice calls, we lose our way.
Yet in that hush, a spark ignites,
A journey leads through endless nights.

So breathe the air that twilight lends,
For here the past and present blends.
With every heartbeat, feel the throng,
Of hidden night where dreams belong.

Spheres of Forgotten Whispers

In realms where echoes softly weave,
The whispers dance, the hearts perceive.
Lost in the mist of timeless lore,
Spheres spin tales, forevermore.

Each sigh a tale from ages past,
In golden hues, the die is cast.
The fragile threads of fate entwine,
In whispered words, our souls align.

With every sound, a memory stirs,
As twilight's breath this night confers.
A moment caught in starlit sighs,
Where dreams take flight beneath the skies.

Beneath the arch of twilight's dome,
The heart seeks paths that lead us home.
To hidden spheres where time stands still,
In whispered tones, we find our will.

So listen close, let silence reign,
In spheres where whispers break the chain.
For in the dark, the light will rise,
And carry dreams beyond the skies.

The Memory of the Silent Road

Upon a path where shadows blend,
A silent road with tales to send.
Each step a memory, soft and clear,
Whispers of journeys linger near.

The trees stand tall, in wisdom old,
Their branches weave the tales untold.
With every breeze, the secrets hum,
The silent road calls, we become.

Footprints linger in the dusk's embrace,
Each trace a moment, a fleeting grace.
In hushed tones, the echoes play,
Guiding us through the waning day.

A tapestry of time and fate,
A winding path, we contemplate.
The memories rise in twilight's weave,
On silent roads, we learn to believe.

So take the step, let shadows dance,
In silent roads, we find our chance.
With open hearts, the journey unfolds,
As memories of life untold.

The Halls of Unsung Melodies

In halls where melodies softly sigh,
The echoes wander, they learn to fly.
Each note a whisper of dreams long past,
In unsung halls, our hearts are cast.

Beneath the arches of twilight's grace,
We find our rhythm, our quiet place.
With every chord, the spirits rise,
Unsung melodies touch the skies.

The laughter lingers in twilight's glow,
A harmony where mysteries flow.
In every corner, the magic hums,
As time is woven, the beauty comes.

So gather close, let voices blend,
In halls where every journey bends.
The unsung songs will guide our way,
Through echoes deep, we joyfully sway.

In melodies that softly weave,
The story calls, we learn to believe.
For in these halls, our spirits soar,
Unsung forever, we seek for more.

Unwritten Stories Beneath the Surface

In whispers soft where secrets lie,
An ocean deep, a silent sigh.
Beneath the waves, the tales unfold,
Of dreams once bright, now lost or sold.

A treasure trove in depths unknown,
With riddles carved on coral stone.
Each current flows with ink of past,
In salty air, the stories cast.

Upon the sand, footprints are traced,
With every step, the past embraced.
The moonlight glints on liquid glass,
While shadows dance, the moments pass.

Yet in the depths, a spark ignites,
A hope reborn in gentle nights.
The waves may crash, but still they soar,
To write anew on every shore.

So gather round, and lend an ear,
For every tale, a world to steer.
In silence deep, the heart can hear,
Unwritten stories—hold them dear.

The Murmur of Ghostly Paths

In twilight's glow, the pathways wind,
Where echoes linger, undefined.
A whispered call through leafy trees,
The breath of time, a tender breeze.

With every step, the shadows play,
As specters dance at end of day.
Their stories etched in cobblestone,
In quiet tones, the past is known.

Beneath the stars, the silence speaks,
In whispered vows and longing peaks.
Forgotten dreams on misty nights,
In silver beams, the ghostly lights.

Through tangled woods, the heart will roam,
To seek the signs of those who've flown.
The murmur calls, a beckoning,
In rustle soft, the echoes sing.

So tread with care on paths once crossed,
For every whisper may hold a cost.
In haunted glades, find what you seek,
The murmurs soft, both kind and bleak.

Shadows of Thought in Darkened Corners

In darkest nooks, where shadows creep,
Lurk thoughts and dreams that we should keep.
A flicker here, a whisper there,
In corners dim, they twirl and flare.

With every thought, a story spins,
Of battles lost and quiet wins.
They swirl like night, a velvet gown,
As stars ignite in silence found.

A flickering flame, a fading spark,
Illuminates the depths so dark.
The weight of fears, the light of hope,
A balance struck, a fragile scope.

Yet in the shroud of starlit night,
The thoughts arise, take swift to flight.
From quiet corners, brave and bold,
The shadows speak, the truth unfolds.

Embrace the shroud, embrace the fear,
For in the dark, the paths are clear.
In shadows' dance, let courage sprout,
The heart will lead when thoughts shout out.

The Echoes Within the Overgrown Garden

In tangled vines where secrets grow,
The garden whispers, soft and slow.
Amidst the blooms, the echoes play,
Of laughter lost in yesterday.

With petals bright and thorns that sting,
The stories weave, the memories cling.
Each fragrant breath an ancient rhyme,
In nature's heart, a dance with time.

The winding paths through wildest dreams,
Are etched in sunlight, kissed by beams.
A symphony of color sings,
In rustling leaves, the joy it brings.

A fountain babbles tales untold,
Of love and loss in shades of gold.
Each ripple catches light anew,
Reflecting hopes in morning dew.

So wander deep where shadows dwell,
Within the garden, hear its spell.
For every echo holds a song,
A timeless truth where hearts belong.

Echoes Lost in the Abyss

In shadows deep, where whispers dwell,
Forgotten tales, they weave a spell.
The night sighs soft, a ghostly tune,
Beneath the watchful eye of the moon.

Waves crash loud on a rocky shore,
Each pulse a heart that beats no more.
A myriad dreams lost in the tide,
Where only echoes of hope abide.

Through fog and mist, the silence reigns,
A dance of light, where darkness strains.
Yet still they call, those voices rare,
To those who dare to stop and care.

The memories drift like autumn leaves,
In laughter's shade, the heart believes.
Though time may steal what once was bright,
The echoes live, eternal light.

So find the path, where shadows part,
Embrace the depth, unveil your heart.
For in the abyss, the lost do find,
The treasures of the hopeful mind.

Maze of Solitude's Song

In tangled paths of empty space,
Each twist a step, a slow embrace.
A song of silence, soft and low,
Where few dare tread, and few may go.

Lost in thought, a mind confined,
The echoes of the heart aligned.
With every choice, a shadow grows,
A haunting tune that no one knows.

Through winding halls of doubt and care,
A whisper floats on the cool night air.
The maze of solitude, a gentle guide,
Leading us where our truths reside.

Yet in the dark, a light will bloom,
A flicker bright, dispelling gloom.
Through each perplexing corner turned,
The song of self is always learned.

Embrace the loneliness with grace,
For in your heart, a sacred place.
With every note, a healing sigh,
In solitude, we learn to fly.

The Veil of Unheard Voices

Behind the veil, where shadows blend,
The whispers of the lost descend.
In muted tones, they weave their dreams,
A tapestry of silent screams.

Each echo soft, a flickering spark,
Igniting truth within the dark.
Of tales unspoken, hearts laid bare,
Traversing skies, where few would dare.

The fragile threads of hope entwine,
In aching hearts, where love divine.
The unseen dance of what could be,
A symphony of mystery.

Yet as we listen, the veil thins fast,
Unheard voices of the past.
They guide us through the labyrinth wide,
To find the peace we long to hide.

So heed the whispers, soft and clear,
For in their song, the truth is near.
Behind the veil, an unseen choice,
Awaits those brave enough to voice.

Secrets Woven in Silence

In quiet corners, secrets dwell,
Woven tight in a fading spell.
Each thread a tale of love and loss,
Entangled dreams, at a heavy cost.

The nights grow long, with shadows clasped,
Each breath a secret tightly grasped.
In whispered tones beneath the star,
The truth reveals just who we are.

Yet silence holds its sacred might,
Where darkness yields to softest light.
In every pause, a heartbeat flows,
A world unseen, where longing grows.

Let not the fear of words unspun,
Deter the heart from what's begun.
For in each secret, beauty lies,
A story told beneath the skies.

So find your voice in hushed refrain,
Unravel tales of joy and pain.
For in the silence, truth will find,
The courage birthed in gentle mind.

Within the Embrace of Hushed Echoes

In twilight's glow, where shadows play,
The whispers dance, then fade away,
A gentle breeze, a feathered sigh,
In quiet realms, our dreams will fly.

Beneath the stars, in silver streams,
We wade through thought, through woven dreams,
Each pulse of night, a heartbeat's call,
A sacred space, where echoes fall.

While time awaits, with bated breath,
In whispered tones, we flirt with death,
The secrets held in silence deep,
Within the heart, our sorrows sleep.

Among the trees, the leaves converse,
With stories old, in verse and verse,
The moonlight bathes the world in grace,
A hidden truth we dare embrace.

In every sigh, a tale is spun,
A tapestry of what's begun,
Within the hush, we find our place,
In echoes soft, we trace our space.

The Tranquil Web of Lost Echoes

In stillness where the shadows blend,
The echoes weave, and softly bend,
A tapestry of nights gone by,
In whispered dreams, no need to cry.

The stars above, they gently hum,
A lullaby of where we're from,
With every note, a heart's refrain,
A soothing balm for every pain.

We walk among the twilight shades,
In secret glades, where light cascades,
Each footstep shared, in silence sweet,
In quiet corners, hearts do meet.

The air is thick with stories told,
In hushed tones, both warm and cold,
The web we build from threads entwined,
A quiet solace, hearts aligned.

So let us linger in this place,
Where echoes fade, yet leave a trace,
A tranquil web of memories spun,
In harmony, we are made one.

The Whispering Threads of Silence

Within the hush, the shadows breathe,
The threads of silence intertwine beneath,
Each whispered note, a fragile sound,
In the stillness, peace is found.

The night unfolds, a velvet hue,
With every star, a wish comes true,
The secrets of the dark impart,
A tender hush, our beating heart.

Through silken strands, our spirits glide,
In whispered threads, we find our guide,
The quiet sighs of who we are,
A gentle pull, a guiding star.

With every breath, the world will pause,
In silence wrapped, we find our cause,
The tender touch of evening's grace,
In whispered threads, we find our place.

Together here, we weave and spin,
The stories dwelled deep within,
In echoes soft, our fears subside,
Through whispering threads, we will confide.

Echoes Entwined in the Stillness

In stillness, echoes softly stir,
A gentle breeze, a whispered blur,
The night unfurls its darkened cloak,
In quietude, our thoughts invoke.

Beneath the moon's ethereal glow,
We find the tales the shadows sow,
With every breath, a tale will swell,
In silenced tones, we learn to tell.

The stars converse in softest light,
As darkness embraces, holds us tight,
In the sacred hush, we carve our way,
With echoes spun from night to day.

Each heartbeat sings a song so rare,
In echo's dance, we shed despair,
Together bound by threads unseen,
In beauty's grip, we drift serene.

So linger here, where silence reigns,
And in the quiet, love remains,
For in this realm, our souls align,
In echoes soft, forever shine.

The Veil of Forgotten Paths

In twilight's embrace the shadows grow,
Old whispers linger where wildflowers sow.
Forgotten echoes dance on the breeze,
Memories entwined in the swaying trees.

Beneath the moon's gaze, the secrets unfold,
A tapestry woven with stories untold.
Each step we take on this winding way,
Reveals the past in a gentle display.

The path may be hidden, but hearts can discern,
The flicker of light where the embers still burn.
With courage to follow the faintest of signs,
We'll unearth the truths that the night defines.

Through mist-covered glades, we weave and we wind,
In search of the treasures that we left behind.
The veil of the past, a shroud fragile and thin,
Calls out to the seekers, inviting them in.

Together we'll wander, a quest to embrace,
Embracing the echoes that time can't erase.
So tread lightly, dear friend, where few have returned,
For the veil of forgotten paths still yearns.

Echoes in the Hushed Corridors

In silent halls where secrets creep,
The shadows linger, the memories seep.
Footsteps soft as the whispering air,
Float through the corridors, vivid and rare.

With every corner, a tale to revive,
In echoes that hum, the past comes alive.
A flickering candle within the cold night,
Illuminates corners that vanish from sight.

The breath of the stories from ages long past,
Lingers in silence, the die has been cast.
Listen closely, for time knows its worth,
In hushed corridors, we uncover our birth.

Drawn to the murmurs that tickle the spine,
In hallowed spaces where shadows entwine.
Unlocking the echoes, we dare to converse,
With specters of wisdom, entwined in the verse.

So wander with me, in this mystical place,
Through whispers and shadows, we'll quicken the pace.
For within the stillness, profound tales await,
In echoes resounding, our hearts resonate.

Secrets Beneath the Shimmering Silence

Beneath the stillness, the waters lie,
Reflecting dreams that evade the eye.
In shimmering silence where ripples fade,
Secrets are kept in the cool, dark shade.

A world underground where shadows play,
Where whispers mingle with night and day.
Each droplet a story, each shimmer a sigh,
Inviting the brave to surface and try.

With eyes wide open to glimmers of truth,
We plunge into depths unguarded by youth.
Searching for fragments of what lay below,
In shimmering silence, the waters will show.

The past is a treasure, both heavy and light,
In echoes of laughter, in shadows of fright.
The depth of the silence can cradle our fears,
As we seek out the secrets that echo through years.

So dive with me deep into waters unknown,
To surface with gems that the heart has outgrown.
For beneath the shimmering, silence reveals,
The magic of life that the heart truly feels.

The Enigma of the Unspoken

In the corners of minds where the silence breeds,
Lie riddles and puzzles, entwined like the reeds.
The unspoken dreams that shiver and writhe,
Crave for the daylight, for words to revive.

A glance, a sigh, a shadow of doubt,
In the spaces between is where truth can sprout.
The enigma dances just out of reach,
A lesson in silence with wisdom to teach.

With hearts wide and eager, the courage we find,
To voice the unsaid, to unravel the mind.
For hope lies entwined in the things left unheard,
In the murmur of feelings that long to be stirred.

So lift up your voice, let the secrets flow free,
For the unspoken tales can set the heart free.
In the canvas of silence, colors emerge,
Painting the stories we're longing to purge.

In this labyrinth where whispers abide,
Let us find the path where our truths can reside.
For in the enigma of what we don't say,
Lies the magic that lights up the way.

The Conundrum of the Quiet Wanderer

In shadows deep, where secrets lie,
A silent path beneath the sky.
With every step, a choice to take,
A conundrum formed, a bond to break.

The moonlight fades, the stars are bright,
In whispering woods where ghosts take flight.
A single breath can shift the way,
The quiet wanderer seeks the day.

With heart in hand, he roams alone,
In search of truths that might be shown.
Each footfall soft, on ancient ground,
A puzzle spins, no solace found.

Yet in the silence, whispers call,
A distant truth, an echo's thrall.
Through tangled roots and thorns so sharp,
He finds a light, a flickering spark.

The wander's path may twist and turn,
But every step invites to learn.
Through secrets held by time's embrace,
The quiet soul shall find his place.

Reflections Through Dimly Lit Halls

In chambers grand, where echoes dwell,
A flicker casts a magic spell.
Reflections dance on marble floors,
Each visage speaks of ancient wars.

With lanterns low, the shadows creep,
While whispered tales begin to seep.
A tapestry of dreams unspooled,
In dimly lit halls, the heart is ruled.

What stories linger in the air,
Of lovers lost, of hearts laid bare?
Their laughter haunts, their sighs remain,
In corridors where joys are pain.

Each corner turned, a ghostly glance,
In fleeting time, they weave their dance.
A mirror's face reflects the past,
In dimly lit halls, the die is cast.

With every step, the past aligns,
In echoes soft, the present shines.
Through walls that speak of love's long call,
We find our place, in timeless thrall.

The Echoes of a Hidden Mirror

In twilight realms where shadows blend,
A hidden mirror bends the end.
It shimmers bright with truths untold,
In silent depths, its stories hold.

Reflections twist, a world apart,
Each glimmer sings a song to heart.
What lies beyond this silver gate?
A whispered fate we contemplate.

Voices rise from depths unseen,
In echoes soft, we search between.
Each gleam unveils a path unclear,
In hidden realms, we shed our fear.

The mirror speaks in riddles vast,
Of dreams once held, of shadows cast.
With every glance, the answers gleam,
The echoes weave the strongest dream.

In quiet moments, hearts can soar,
Through hidden mirrors, seek for more.
For every truth, a lesson learned,
In echoes deep, our fate discerned.

A Voyage into the Whispering Unknown

Upon a ship of starlit sails,
We journey forth where whispers wail.
The ocean's breath, a lullaby,
Calls forth the hearts that yearn to fly.

In waves that crash with mighty cry,
The secrets deep, they beckon nigh.
A voyage laced with dreams untold,
Into the unknown, brave and bold.

With every swell, the stars align,
The compass spins, a path divine.
What treasures wait beneath the foam?
In whispered tales, we find our home.

With spirits high, the sails unfurled,
We sail beyond the known, the world.
Each twist and turn, a chance to learn,
In whispering winds, our souls do yearn.

So let us drift on currents strange,
In search of wonders that may change.
For in the unknown, dreams take flight,
A voyage grand through endless night.

Notes Unplayed in the Shy Twilight

In the hush where shadows creep,
A melody begins to weep.
Soft flickers of a fading light,
Whisper secrets of the night.

Ghostly echoes fill the air,
Each note caught in twilight's snare.
They dance like fireflies in gloom,
Awaiting keys to stir their bloom.

Locked away in silence deep,
UNheard dreams in stillness sleep.
Fingers hover, longing grace,
To set free this hidden place.

With every breath, a hope takes flight,
In the canvas of the night.
Let the music find its way,
To touch the dawn of a new day.

In the twilight's gentle sway,
All unplayed notes begin to play.
Through the silence, hear them call,
A symphony that binds us all.

The Choreography of Silent Steps

In the depths of moonlit grace,
Footprints weave in secret space.
Each soft patter, a tale untold,
Of worlds hidden, yet so bold.

A cadence forms on cobbled stone,
Where whispers dance and shadows moan.
Silence drapes a velvet veil,
Cradling hopes that never pale.

Twisting paths beneath the stars,
Journey marked by silent scars.
In unseen rhythms, spirits glide,
While dreams and wishes gently bide.

When the night begins to break,
The stillness bends, the heart will quake.
For every step that's softly pressed,
Reveals the truth we long invest.

With each breath, a chance to fly,
In the quiet, hearts defy.
The choreography unfolds,
As courage warms the night with gold.

Whispers in the Winding Maze

Through twisting turns and narrow paths,
Echoes hold their secret baths.
Whispers curl like misty sighs,
Where shadows wink and daylight cries.

In the maze where time stands still,
Each corner bends with gentle thrill.
Soft murmurs beckon from the dark,
That spark the heart to leave a mark.

Veils of silence, cloaked in night,
Guide the lost towards the light.
With every step, a hint bestowed,
Leading souls along the road.

In paths unseen, the spirits roam,
Calling forth the weary home.
Inturning moments, wisdom sings,
Of hidden truths the journey brings.

Listen close to what's unspoken,
In the quiet, no vow's broken.
For every whisper holds a dream,
Flowing like a silver stream.

Shadows of the Unheard Journey

In the dusk where silence dwells,
Footsteps echo, softly tells.
Shadows rise as night unfurls,
Wrapping tales of distant swirls.

A journey marked by unseen lines,
Where hope and fear in stillness twine.
Each moment holds a breath concealed,
In hidden paths, our fates revealed.

Between the worlds of dark and light,
The dance of fate begins its flight.
With every heartbeat, stories weave,
Of dreams once lost, now to believe.

In shadows long, the memories play,
Guiding souls along the way.
Though no one hears the whispers low,
In silent journeys, hearts must grow.

Embrace the paths that twist and fade,
For in the night, new dreams are made.
Shadows speak what eyes can't see,
In the journey, there lies the key.

When Silence Speaks in Shadows

In twilight's hush, where whispers cling,
The shadows dance, and secrets sing.
A story floats on fragile air,
In stillness wrapped, a silent prayer.

Soft footsteps tread on ancient ground,
Where echoes of the past are found.
The moonlight weaves through branches bare,
And dreams unfurl, beyond despair.

In every glance, a tale unfolds,
Of moments caught, and courage bold.
The heart beats softly, knowing why,
In silence, truths begin to fly.

As every sigh meets gentle night,
In darkness blooms a hidden light.
The world holds breath, in calm belief,
For silence speaks, its own motif.

The shadows fade, as dawn awakes,
With whispers lost in morning's breaks.
Yet echoes linger, soft and low,
In every soul, the shadows glow.

The Forgotten Music of the Heart

Beneath the stars, a melody plays,
A tune forgotten in endless days.
Each note, a whisper of the soul,
Reminds us of what makes us whole.

In quiet moments, it will rise,
A song unseen by longing eyes.
With every heartbeat, softly strummed,
The music of the heart becomes.

When shadows gather, and hope is dim,
The silent chords begin to brim.
They dance like fireflies in the dark,
Rekindling dreams, igniting spark.

Through tangled paths, we seek to find,
The rhythm lost, a melody blind.
Yet in the silence, it still waits,
To weave its way through heaven's gates.

So listen close, and let it start,
The symphony within your heart.
For in the hush of night, we see,
The forgotten music sets us free.

Reverberations of the Unheard Journey

Across the lands, where footsteps roam,
An unseen path leads us back home.
With every turn, a voice will call,
In echoes bound, we rise and fall.

The whispers of the road unfold,
In stories etched, in shadows told.
Each bend a choice, each pause a chance,
To dance with dreams in wild romance.

In every silence, we shall find,
The traces left by hearts combined.
For journeys taken, though unseen,
Are woven deep in all that's been.

The stars above still trace the way,
Through darkest nights to dawning day.
A call to wander, explore the vast,
To find the love that holds us fast.

So hear the rhythms of the past,
In every breath, our shadows cast.
The uncharted paths await our feet,
On this grand journey, love's heartbeat.

Subtle Echoes in the Night

In velvet skies, the stars awake,
As echoes stir, the silence shakes.
Beneath the hush, the world will sigh,
In gentle whispers, the dreams fly high.

The moonlit paths, so soft and bright,
Guide weary hearts through tranquil night.
Each secret shared in quiet grace,
Illuminates the hidden space.

With every rustle, shadows speak,
In subtle tones, the answers seek.
The night unfolds its tender charm,
Enveloping all in sweet warm calm.

As hearts align with nature's tune,
The echoes rise, beneath the moon.
In tranquil breaths, the spirit flows,
Through subtle hints, the truth bestows.

So wander forth, beneath starlight's glow,
Let echoes guide the way you go.
For in the night, hope's whispers soar,
Embracing you, forevermore.

The Untold Paths of the Mute Traveler

In quiet corners where shadows dwell,
A traveler walks, with stories to tell.
Though words won't flow from their silent lips,
Each step reveals a world in scripts.

With eyes like lanterns, they pierce the night,
Unseen realms bathed in silver light.
Their heart, a compass, seeking the true,
In whispers of dreams that once they knew.

Paths twist and turn in a woven dance,
Where hope and sorrow share a glance.
Each silent moment holds magic rare,
A tapestry rich, spun from thin air.

The stars listen closely; they know the way,
To map the silence, come what may.
In every heartbeat, a language grows,
The untold paths, where no one goes.

A realm of colors, unseen by all,
Where echoes of laughter rise and fall.
This journey of one, a saga untold,
In the heart of the mute, a legend bold.

Whispers Through the Fog

In the early dawn, when the mist drapes low,
Whispers emerge, soft and slow.
Secrets carried on the chilling breeze,
Tales of the night, shared with the trees.

Figures dance in the shrouded gray,
As the world awakens, in hesitant sway.
Voices of spirits, long since passed,
Calling through time, their shadows cast.

With every gust that brushes the ground,
Ancient stories can still be found.
Echoes of laughter, or sighs of despair,
Fragmented pieces floating in air.

The fog wraps close like an old friend,
Binding the lost, till the journey's end.
Murmurs entwined with the song of the sea,
In this foggy embrace, we find harmony.

Through the swirling haze, hope flickers bright,
A beacon of warmth in the fold of the night.
For every whisper, a chance to connect,
In whispers through the fog, we reflect.

A Journey Through Muffled Memories

In faded corners of distant days,
Lie buried treasures of fractured rays.
Muffled whispers trace paths of the past,
A journey through time, shadows cast.

Fleeting glimpses of laughter and tears,
Echoes that linger, remind us of years.
Through the silence, a heartbeat calls,
Resonating soft through forgotten walls.

Worn photographs, a sepia dream,
In every pixel, a flickering gleam.
Memories dance in a quiet refrain,
Each step on the path, a sweet ache and pain.

The air grows heavy with stories unsaid,
Of voices that linger, though long since fled.
In the tapestry woven by light and by dark,
A journey unfolds, igniting the spark.

With each pondered moment, we begin to see,
The beauty of what used to be free.
In muffled memories, we find our way,
Past shadows that shape us, night into day.

The Shadowed Passage of Lost Voices

In the shadowed passage where silence thrives,
Lost voices echo, where memory survives.
Their whispers curl like smoke in the air,
Longing to be heard, but found everywhere.

Steps tread softly on cobbled stone,
Guided by ghosts, forever alone.
Navigating turns, where secrets hide,
In the depth of silence, they bide.

Each heart carries tales of what once was,
In the quiet dark, a gentle pause.
Reverberating through chambers of time,
The shadowed passage, a haunting rhyme.

Through the depths of night, hopes intertwine,
In whispers, von memories softly align.
A meeting of lives, both lost and found,
In the passage of shadows, we are unbound.

So linger awhile, let the silence speak,
For in each lost voice, there's solace to seek.
Through the veils of twilight, we learn to trust,
In the shadowed passage, our dreams adjust.

Paths Untold Beneath the Stars

In twilight's grasp, the shadows roam,
Where secrets whisper, far from home.
The starlit paths, so faintly drawn,
Lead weary hearts to the break of dawn.

With echoes of dreams, lost and found,
Each step echoes on hallowed ground.
The nightingale sings of journeys started,
While luminous tales of the brave-hearted.

Through glades untouched by time's cruel hand,
Lie stories woven through enchanted land.
Each pebble glints with history's spark,
Guiding the seekers who dare to embark.

In breaths held close, magic ignites,
Unraveling threads of forgotten sights.
The moon casts light on the paths we tread,
A guide for the souls who follow the thread.

So venture forth where the wild winds blow,
To realms where the unknown begins to glow.
For beneath the stars, a truth unfolds,
In paths untold, our fate bravely holds.

The Stillness Between Breaths

In moments caught, we pause and dwell,
Amidst the chaos, an untold spell.
The silence hums a secret tune,
Beneath the watchful, silver moon.

What dreams emerge from the quiet space,
Where time expands, and fears erase?
A heartbeat's rhythm, soft as lace,
Embraces the stillness, a warm embrace.

In every sigh and whispered prayer,
Lies a promise woven in the air.
The world spins on, yet here we stand,
In tranquil grace, with outstretched hands.

The echo of thoughts, like ripples spread,
In stillness, the shadows of doubt are shed.
A flicker of hope in gossamer light,
Illuminates paths once shrouded in night.

As life rushes on, remember this place,
Where stillness lingers, timeless, and grace.
In-between breaths, we find our way,
To the heart of magic, come what may.

The Riddle of the Unseen Corners

In corners shadowed, riddles dwell,
Whispers of secrets, a timeless spell.
Each step we take, a clue to find,
The hidden truths that guide the blind.

With candlelight flickering in the night,
We trace the edges, the dimming light.
Where laughter echoes, and shadows dance,
Lost in the game of a fleeting chance.

A tapestry woven with threads of fate,
Glimmers of hope in each twisted gate.
Curious hearts seek what's yet to see,
The mysteries locked in the shadows, free.

What lies beyond the curtains drawn?
A phantasmagoria, a world reborn.
In whispered riddles, the truth will sing,
Of unseen corners and forgotten things.

So wander forth with eyes wide bright,
For in silence awaits the guiding light.
Embrace the enigma, let it unfold,
Discover the riddles, both young and old.

Woven Silences in the Twisted Maze

In twisted paths, the silence weaves,
A labyrinth where each heart believes.
Through echoes lost, we seek to find,
The woven thread that binds the mind.

With careful steps, we navigate,
The shadows dance, and fate awaits.
Each turn reveals a tale untold,
In the silence, our courage unfolds.

The air thick with secrets, shared in grace,
In the stillness of this forgotten place.
Fragrant with promise, the night holds close,
The beauty found in the hush we chose.

With every heartbeat, a new path drawn,
Guided by whispers of a brand new dawn.
In this twisted maze, our spirits soar,
As woven silences open the door.

So step within, with heart held high,
Through tangled dreams, we learn to fly.
For in the silence, magic lies,
In tangled paths, we find the skies.

Whispers in the Forgotten Maze

In shadows deep where secrets weave,
The silent paths of ghosts believe.
Each twist and turn, a breath concealed,
In echoes where the heartstrings healed.

With every step the whispers bite,
Of dreams long lost beneath the night.
A flicker there, a fleeting sound,
In haunted theme, lost hopes are found.

In twilight's grasp, the shadows loom,
As time stands still within the gloom.
The maze enshrined in foggy haze,
Where memories dance in soft malaise.

Through tangled roots and whispers frail,
The stories twist, the voices wail.
In beating hearts, the echoes swell,
Of lives once lived, of darkened spell.

Yet in the depths of tangled fate,
A single truth can resonate.
When courage stirs and paths are cleared,
The light will shine, the maze revered.

Shadows of Unspoken Truths

Beneath the surface, silence dwarfs,
In shadows where the light departs.
The heart whispers, the mind confides,
In every glance, the secret hides.

The weight of words can crush the chest,
While silence shields the truth's unrest.
Each moment holds a tale untold,
In glances shared, in hands we hold.

Yet bravely borne, the whispers call,
Through unseen walls, we hear their thrall.
They weave a tapestry of fate,
Of bonds unseen, of love innate.

In realms where shadows twist and turn,
A flickering light ignites the burn.
When hearts unite and courage greets,
The truths emerge where silence meets.

So tread lightly through the veils of night,
For shadows harbor hidden light.
With every heartbeat, we confess,
In whispers soft, we seek to bless.

The Enigma of Quiet Pathways

In tranquil corners, secrets dwell,
In pathways quiet, thoughts compel.
The rustling leaves share silent tales,
Of journeys bound by whispered trails.

Each footfall soft, a dance with fate,
As nature sways, the soul awaits.
In labyrinths of wood and stone,
The echoes fade, yet still are known.

With every turn, the dusk unfurls,
As twilight folds in muted swirls.
A flicker bright through darkened trees,
Awakens dreams with gentle pleas.

The heart knows well the quiet tune,
That hums along with silver moon.
In shadowed paths, we find our grace,
In every pause, a warm embrace.

So linger here, where peace resides,
In whispers soft, the spirit guides.
Each quiet step, a leap of trust,
In nature's arms, return to rust.

Reverberations in Stillness

In stillness bright where echoes play,
The world around drifts far away.
Each moment's pause, a breath arrives,
As silence stirs, the spirit thrives.

With gentle hands, the time unfolds,
A symphony of tales retold.
In hushed refrain, the heart complies,
Through whispered winds, the soul replies.

The ripples dance on tranquil streams,
Where shadows shift in waking dreams.
Their subtle sway, a fleeting glance,
In quietude, hearts learn to dance.

Yet within this calm, a tempest brews,
The passion hides in tender hues.
When stillness reigns, the truth ignites,
In resonant waves, the heart takes flight.

So linger here, where silence reigns,
In whispered thoughts, the love remains.
For in the void, where echoes blend,
We softly find the strength to mend.

In the Wake of Muffled Whispers

In shadows deep where secrets sway,
The wisps of sound drift softly away.
A fleeting sigh, a distant call,
In hushed embraces, the moments fall.

The trees stand tall, their branches bare,
Guarding tales that linger in air.
A phantom's laugh, a gentle breeze,
Whispers echo beneath the leaves.

With every glance, the stories twist,
Into the realms of shadows mist.
The past entwines with threads of fate,
In velvet nights, we contemplate.

Beneath the stars, the echoes play,
In stillness wrapped, they dance and sway.
Each word a sigh, each silence loud,
In the wake of whispers, shadows bowed.

Those ghostly sounds, like summer rain,
Awake the heart, yet soothe the pain.
In dreams, they flutter, soft and light,
Muffled whispers, lost in night.

The Shroud of Quiet Descent

A cloak of night, a shroud of grey,
Falls ever softly, as dusk gives way.
The world retreats, as shadows merge,
In hush of twilight, we quietly surge.

Beneath the stars, the secrets hide,
In whispered tones, they gently glide.
The calm enfolds like a tender sigh,
As dreams take flight in the endless sky.

The moonlight weaves a silver thread,
Through leafy boughs where spirits tread.
A tranquil stream, a secret place,
Invites the heart to slow its pace.

In quiet realms, we hear the song,
Of nature's pulse, where we belong.
The shroud descends, a soft embrace,
Instilling peace, a timeless grace.

So wander forth, through night's delight,
In shadows cloaked, love's purest light.
For in the stillness, we are blessed,
In quiet descent, we find our rest.

Haunting Melodies of the Void

In still of night, the echoes rise,
A haunting tune that never dies.
Through empty halls and barren skies,
Melodies weave where silence lies.

Each note a wish, a longing plea,
Wandering through the realm of dreams.
In twilight's grasp, they dance and flee,
A tapestry of whispered themes.

The shadows hum a ghostly song,
Yet rhythm flows where hearts belong.
In every beat, a story spun,
A haunting dance, two souls as one.

The void resounds with every breath,
As echoes taunt the grip of death.
Yet in this space, we find our voice,
In haunting melodies, we rejoice.

So listen close, let spirits guide,
Through chords of loss and love's great tide.
In every sigh, in every mood,
Haunting melodies softly brood.

Echoing Thoughts Through Dim Paths

Beneath the boughs where shadows creep,
Whispers of dreams in silence sleep.
Each thought a spark, a flickering flame,
Echoing softly, calling your name.

Through dim-lit paths, we wander wide,
In search of light, where secrets bide.
With every step, the echoes grow,
Guiding us where we long to go.

The grey of dusk unveils the heart,
In every pause, the echoes start.
A gentle breeze carries the past,
While shadows stretch, and moments last.

In twilight's glow, reflections gleam,
Whispers entwined in every dream.
Thoughts like lanterns on a stream,
Illuminate the night's soft seam.

So follow forth, dear traveler brave,
Through echoes soft, let memories pave.
For in the dim, where silence reigns,
Your heart will know what love sustains.

The Unseen Tapestry of Sound

In shadows spun of whispered threads,
A melody of silence spreads.
From hidden wells of thought it flows,
It dances softly, none can know.

A lullaby beneath the stars,
Where echoes heal invisible scars.
The heart, a drum that beats untold,
In every note, a story bold.

Through hallowed halls where secrets swell,
A symphony of dreams to tell.
Each fleeting sound, a fleeting glance,
In time's embrace, we weave our dance.

In corners dim, where shadows breathe,
The soundless songs begin to wreathe.
A tapestry of starlit flight,
Unseen by day, revealed by night.

So let us listen, soft and clear,
To every ghost we hold so dear.
For in the silence, truth takes wing,
And every heart can learn to sing.

Hidden Depths of Muted Reflections

In waters deep, where stillness lies,
The echoes of forgotten sighs.
Each ripple holds a tale concealed,
A mystery yet to be revealed.

Beneath the surface, shadows sway,
With every glance, they slip away.
A silent dance of fleeting light,
Where secrets murmur, soft as night.

In pools of thought, the past remains,
Within each drop, a world contains.
The weight of time, a gentle press,
In whispered dreams, we find our rest.

Reflections cast in muted hue,
Of lives once lived and love so true.
As twilight deepens, visions steep,
In depths of silence, we shall keep.

So let us dive, with faith anew,
Where echoes old, the heart breaks through.
For in the depths, we find our grace,
A tapestry of time and place.

The Quiet Dance of Forgotten Dreams

In twilight's glow, where shadows wane,
The dreams of yesteryears remain.
They float like whispers on the breeze,
In secret corners, hearts at ease.

Each memory, a ghostly trace,
A hymn of love, a soft embrace.
The starlit sky, a canvas bare,
Awakens hopes in midnight air.

In silent rooms where echoes play,
Forgotten dreams still find their way.
They twirl like leaves on autumn ground,
In solitude, their joy is found.

So let us join this gentle waltz,
With every step, the heart exalts.
For in this dance of shades and light,
Forgotten dreams take flight, take flight.

In quiet moments, we shall see,
The beauty in our memory.
For every dream that graced our nights,
Still dances in the soft starlights.

Whispers Among the Wandering Stones

Amidst the rocks where secrets lie,
The whispers of the ages sigh.
Each stone a tale that time forgot,
A journey marked by every spot.

They speak of dreams entwined with fate,
In silent echoes, calm and great.
As winds of time weave through the ages,
Their stories dance on ancient pages.

Beneath the moon, when shadows roam,
The stones will sing of hearth and home.
Their voices blend, a choir low,
A song of earth, a timeless flow.

So sit awhile, and hear them call,
The whispers rise, the echoes fall.
In every crack, a wisdom shared,
A tapestry of love, declared.

In wandering paths where wisdom grows,
The heart can feel what nature knows.
For every stone holds tales untold,
A legacy of dreams, so bold.

The Cloistered Pathways of Thought

In corridors where dreams might hide,
Shadows linger, mysteries abide.
Gentle echoes of a time long past,
Whispers of wisdom that forever last.

Winding paths through the bramble of night,
Each step reveals a spark of light.
Truths entwined with threads of fate,
Unraveling secrets, oh, don't wait.

A forest of questions, swirling fog,
Lost in the maze like an old, tired dog.
Glimmers of laughter break through the gloom,
Hope ignites like a flower in bloom.

The heart beats softly, guiding the way,
Through hidden doors where dreams sway.
In silent chambers, thoughts collide,
Here lie the futures that we've denied.

So wander freely, let your mind soar,
In the cloistered pathways, find evermore.
Embrace the wonder that lies ahead,
A tapestry of words where fears have fled.

Ramparts of the Faded Reverie

Upon the hill, where shadows creep,
Stands a fortress, the past so deep.
Walls of memory, sturdy and high,
Guarding dreams that fade and die.

Worn stones speak of laughter and tears,
Echoes of joy mingled with fears.
In the twilight, secrets unveil,
Life's sweet stories linger and sail.

Each crack in the waft of the veil,
Holds a whisper of lost tales.
Time's embrace in the dawn's warm glow,
Mends the spirits that used to flow.

From ramparts high, look down below,
See the embers of love's gentle glow.
In fading colors, the heart's refrain,
Awakens hope from the shadows' chain.

So let us wander this hallowed ground,
Where the echoes of the heart resound.
In faded reverie, find our bliss,
A dance of dreams in a silken mist.

The Spiral of Unseen Voices

Spiraling thoughts, a dance of air,
Whispers weave through the weightless glare.
Hear the tunes of the winds that sigh,
Notes of wonder as they drift by.

Unseen voices, calling from afar,
Drawn to the light of a distant star.
A melody soft, the heartstrings pluck,
Guiding lost souls, lending them luck.

In the twilight, the dreams intertwine,
A tapestry rich, the threads divine.
Through realms where the spirits entwine,
Laughter echoes, a song so fine.

Like petals swirling in summer's breeze,
Each moment captured, a fleeting tease.
In the spiral, we lift and glide,
To where time merges, and hearts abide.

So let the voices lead you on,
In the world where the past is gone.
With every step, the magic's near,
Embrace the gifts of what you hear.

Silent Whispers in the Dark

In the stillness where shadows loom,
Silent whispers banish the gloom.
Soft secrets painted in the night,
Hold the echoes of lost delight.

Beneath the stars, where dreams take flight,
Gentle murmurs throughout the night.
Nature's lullaby, pure and sweet,
Guides the weary with calm heartbeat.

Each breath held close, a hidden spark,
In the silence, there lies no mark.
A world unseen, in whispers confide,
Tales of magic the night will provide.

So listen closely, let your heart sing,
To the secrets the night breeze brings.
In silent whispers, hope's flame ignites,
A journey begins under starlit nights.

In this cathedral of shadowy grace,
Find solace, a warm embrace.
For in the dark, dreams softly glide,
Here in the quiet, hope will abide.

Footsteps in the Ghostly Labyrinth

In twilight's grip, the shadows tread,
Whispers linger where no words are said.
Turn down the path, where lost dreams dwell,
Each heartbeat echoes, a secret to tell.

The moonlight dances on cobblestone,
Guiding the way for the heart alone.
Winding corridors of hopes long past,
Footsteps trace tales, shadows cast.

A flicker of lantern, a spectral call,
Promises made in the depths of the hall.
Through the haze, a glimmer of light,
In the haunting stillness, something ignites.

Dare we explore what history hides?
In the heart of the maze, our courage abides.
With every turn, a memory awakens,
Footsteps intrepid, the spirit unshaken.

As twilight surrenders to evening's embrace,
We wander deeper in this enchanted space.
The labyrinth breathes, alive with the past,
Footsteps in twilight, forever steadfast.

The Forgotten Echo Chamber

In a chamber draped in shadows old,
Echoes of laughter start to unfold.
Whispers of secrets, lost in the air,
Memories lingering, heavy with care.

Walls lined with whispers of tales once spun,
Echoes of joy when the day was young.
Footsteps forgotten, yet strikingly clear,
In the heart of silence, the past draws near.

A single note, like a candle's flame,
Illuminates hopes, yet whispers a name.
Through corridors vast where echoes reside,
The heart finds solace, the soul's gentle guide.

In rhythmic pulses, the silence breathes,
A song of the heart in the chamber seethes.
With every beat, the echoes will rise,
Stories unraveled beneath starlit skies.

When the world feels weightless, and moments congeal,
The chamber awakens, and time learns to heal.
In echoes of whispers, the soul feels freed,
An orchestra playing, a melody's creed.

Chasing Shadows in the Stillness

In the hush of night, shadows dance free,
Chasing the flicker of what could be.
Silvery moonlight spills on the ground,
Whispers of dreams in the air abound.

Through the stillness, a sigh weaves tight,
A gentle embrace, a caress of light.
Twisting and turning, we follow the call,
Chasing the shadows that flicker and fall.

In each heartbeat, the silence will sing,
A symphony woven from fragile string.
Hopes take flight in the cool night air,
Chasing the shadows, we shed every care.

A tapestry spun from laughter and tears,
We grasp at the shadows, we conquer our fears.
In the stillness of night, a promise is made,
Chasing the essence of dreams that won't fade.

As dawn draws close, the shadows retreat,
But their whispers endure, so tender and sweet.
Chasing the echoes that linger behind,
In the stillness of life, true magic we find.

Veils of Echoing Silence

In the dawn's embrace, the silence unfolds,
Veils woven softly, in secrets enfold.
Beneath the surface, a world waits in gray,
Echoing whispers where shadows play.

In the fabric of time, each thread tells a tale,
Of dreams unchained, of hopes that unveil.
With every heartbeat, the silence reflects,
Veils of emotion, in stillness, connects.

In the heart of the quiet, a truth lies concealed,
The hush of the moment, never revealed.
Veils flutter gently, like whispers in space,
Echoing silence, a warm embrace.

Through corridors soft, the echoes retreat,
In the depths of the quiet, our souls find their beat.
Awash in the calm, we learn how to see,
Veils of echoing silence, setting us free.

With a breath held dear, we linger awhile,
In the veils of the silence, we find our own style.
As day breaks anew, the whispers take flight,
In the echoing silence, we find our true light.

Silence Beneath the Twisting Arches

Beneath the arches, silence sighs,
Where whispers dance in shadows shy.
Midst ancient stones that hold the night,
The magic stirs, a soft delight.

Forgotten tales in echoes dwell,
Where secrets weave a sleepy spell.
The twilight paints on cobblestones,
Its quiet brush, a language known.

In corners dark, the shadows play,
They twist and turn, then fade away.
A fleeting glimpse of bygone dreams,
In silence rich, the starlight beams.

Underneath the archways high,
A slumbering world, tucked away nigh.
With every breath, the stillness grows,
As ancient paths in silence flow.

And when the moon begins to rise,
The night's embrace, soft lullabies.
Beneath those arches, lost in time,
The heartbeats match a whispered rhyme.

Between the Folds of Still Air

In stillness wrapped, the world unfolds,
Between the whispers, stories told.
A breeze, a sigh, as soft as silk,
The ceaseless dance, like waves of milk.

Amid the folds where shadows creep,
The secrets hold, their vigil keep.
Time lingers on, a gentle hand,
Where echoes map the silent land.

As twilight drapes in velvet blue,
The stars appear, come out anew.
With every breath, the hush befalls,
And dreams float high on silken thralls.

The stillness speaks, a language rare,
In every sigh, a tale laid bare.
Between the folds of quiet night,
The unseen realms reclaim their light.

And in that space where magic stirs,
A heartbeat quickens, softly whirs.
Left in the hush, we find ourselves,
In stillness deep, the soul's own shelves.

Paths Intertwined with Shadows

Along the paths where shadows meet,
A world unseen, mysterious yet sweet.
Footsteps trace on cobbled ways,
In every turn, a secret plays.

The night unfurls its velvet coat,
Where whispers weave and dreams emote.
With every step, the shadows blend,
In tales of yore, where journeys bend.

Through twirling leaves that catch the light,
The paths diverge, and rejoin with night.
Each twist and turn reveals anew,
A haunting past that beckons true.

With arms outstretched, the darkness calls,
In play of light, as twilight falls.
The roads entwined like lovers' fate,
A tapestry that can't sedate.

And as the moon begins to rise,
The starlit truth ignites the skies.
Pathways carved in shadows bold,
The story weaves; the night unfolds.

The Secret Chorus of Obscured Souls

In shadows cast by evening's glow,
The secret chorus starts to flow.
A symphony of whispered sighs,
Among the stars, their song defies.

The echoes dance on winds' embrace,
In twilight's calm, they find their place.
Each note entwined with sacred night,
A haunting tune, a pure delight.

As flickers stir in night's domain,
The music swells like gentle rain.
These souls obscure, yet brightly gleam,
In harmony, they weave a dream.

Beneath the moon's benevolent gaze,
They sing of life, through misty haze.
And in their song, our hearts align,
Lost to the world, we intertwine.

The secret chorus, veiled by time,
In every beat, a whispered rhyme.
As shadows blend, their voices rise,
A melody that never dies.

The Sanctuary of Muted Secrets

In the shadows where whispers dwell,
Lies a tale only silence can tell.
Dusty tomes and forgotten lore,
Guard the secrets of those who explore.

Ancient echoes linger in air,
Remnants of wishes and gentle despair.
Time stands still in this sacred place,
Veiled in twilight, wrapped in grace.

Underneath the gnarled old tree,
Hidden treasures, elusive and free.
With every rustle, a story unfolds,
In quiet corners, the heart gently holds.

Moonlight dances upon each wall,
Illuminating secrets that softly call.
In the stillness, truth finds its way,
To weave a tapestry of night and day.

So return to the hush where dreams take flight,
In this sanctuary, where shadows ignite.
With reverence, seek what's deeply entwined,
In the whispers of souls, the heart of mankind.

The Dance of Unvoiced Dreams

Once upon a fleeting night,
Where stars shimmer with quiet light.
Phantoms twirl in a waltz so grand,
Guided by the dreams they planned.

A breath of wind whispers a tune,
Rising softly like a silver moon.
In the silence, magic takes its form,
A hidden dance in the gentle storm.

Figures glide through the unseen haze,
Their movements a hymn, a lover's praise.
In the shadows, stories conspire,
As unspoken hopes ignite a fire.

Every twirl and sway, a promise made,
In a world where fears gradually fade.
With each step, an untouched theme,
As if we're lost within a dream.

So linger here, where wishes weave,
In the unvoiced dreams that we believe.
In their depths, a truth lies awake,
A dance of souls, for love's sweet sake.

When Footsteps Fade into Stillness

In the forest where echoes cease,
Footfalls whisper, then find peace.
Leaves, like specters, softly sigh,
Beneath the vast, unyielding sky.

Moments linger, suspended in time,
Each heartbeat a gentle chime.
Distance swells, a quiet refrain,
As whispers fade like drops of rain.

The path is etched with dreams once bold,
Now mere shadows, stories untold.
Yet every silence holds a trace,
Of fleeting joys, and love's embrace.

Where the heartbeats begin to slow,
And memories fade like melting snow.
In the breath of night, solace is found,
When footsteps fade without a sound.

So walk with care through twilight's haze,
Embrace the stillness, let it amaze.
For in the calm, beauty resides,
When footsteps fade, the spirit abides.

Tracing the Invisible Veins

In the fabric of dusk, threads intertwine,
Whispers of magic, subtle and fine.
Paths not taken, yet softly known,
Reveal the journeys that we've outgrown.

Veins of the world, invisible flow,
Carrying stories, depths we don't show.
With each heartbeat, a connection appears,
Binding the dreams with laughter and tears.

Through the silence, the pulse remains,
Mapping the joy, the loss, the gains.
Undercurrents of fate, unseen maps,
Guide us through life with gentle taps.

In every breath, a tale we share,
A tapestry woven from love and care.
We live as one, though apart we seem,
Tracing the veins of a collective dream.

So listen closely to what's not said,
In the spaces between, where visions are bred.
For life's true magic lies in the seams,
As we trace together our intertwined dreams.

The Quiet Heart of the Maze

In shadows deep, where whispers play,
A labyrinth of dreams awaits the day.
With every turn, a choice to make,
The heart's soft call, a gentle quake.

Beneath the arch of ivy's grasp,
A silent truth, within our clasp.
Each winding path, a story spun,
Of courage found and battles won.

In hidden corners, secrets dwell,
In echoes long, where silence fell.
A spark of hope in darkened halls,
The quiet heart, its rhythm calls.

As stars align above the maze,
We trace our steps, lost in a haze.
Yet, through the mist, our spirits steer,
The quiet heart, forever near.

Secrets Hidden in Still Waters

Beneath the glassy surface lie,
Whispers of the earth and sky.
The dance of leaves in twilight's breath,
A symphony that exclaims of death.

Yet in the depths, a truth unfolds,
The tales of life, of brave and bold.
Each droplet holds a world untold,
A mystery in silence behold.

Fish dart past, like thoughts in flight,
Reflecting moon and starlit night.
A mirror cast, both wise and deep,
Where secrets rest in quiet sleep.

In every ripple, shadows play,
Floating dreams that drift away.
The still waters, a calm embrace,
Concealing time and space.

The Mystery of the Silent Wanderer

A figure cloaked in twilight's hue,
Moves softly where the wildflowers grew.
Footsteps blend with whispers fine,
A story woven, thread by line.

No words are spoken, yet we feel,
A pulse of life, a silent reel.
Eyes that hold the night's own grace,
In quiet gardens, there's a place.

Through silver mist, the wanderer glides,
A keeper of the secrets he hides.
Where shadows stretch and sunsets burn,
The mystery fades, but hearts still yearn.

In every glance, a tale sown,
In whispers soft, we find our own.
The silent wanderer drifts afar,
A guiding light, a distant star.

The Path of Silent Reflections

On winding paths through tranquil woods,
Where silence speaks, and patience broods.
The trees entwine in green embrace,
A sacred space, a hidden place.

With every step, the world will change,
A mirror's touch, serene and strange.
In gentle light, the shadows weave,
A tapestry, of what we believe.

Each pause reveals the heart's own tune,
In harmony with sun and moon.
We walk in thought, unspoken dreams,
The path unfolds in silver streams.

The air is thick with quiet truth,
The echoes fade from distant youth.
Along this route of soft affections,
We find our way in silent reflections.

Threads of Silence in the Weave of Time

In shadows deep, where whispers dwell,
The threads of silence weave their spell.
Each moment stitched, with care and grace,
A tapestry of time we trace.

The loom it creaks, a gentle sigh,
As memories drift, like clouds on high.
A tapestry of faded dreams,
Unraveling in soft moonbeams.

Within this weave, our stories blend,
Each thread a life, each knot a friend.
Together sewn, through laughter, pain,
A fabric rich, that will remain.

In echoes soft, the past will call,
As time weaves on, we stand, we fall.
Threads of silence, strong and taut,
In every heart, a lesson taught.

So hold your dreams, let silence speak,
In woven paths, it's truth we seek.
For in the fabric, we find our place,
In threads of silence, time's embrace.

The Echoing Heart of Time's Maze

In corridors where shadows play,
The echoes of lost moments sway.
A heart that beats in rhythmic rhyme,
Resounds within the maze of time.

Each turn reveals a hidden door,
Leading us to dreams of yore.
With whispered winds, we tread the path,
Through joy, through sorrow, love, and wrath.

The candles flicker, soft and bright,
Illuminating dreams each night.
In every corner, secrets lie,
Waiting for the brave to try.

And in the heart, a knowledge swells,
With stories only time compels.
Through twisting turns, we seek the light,
In echoes that embrace the night.

So journey on through winding ways,
Embrace the maze, let time amaze.
For in each echo, truth shall wane,
A heart that knows both joy and pain.

When Dreams Fade into Quietude

In twilight hues, where shadows blend,
Whispers of dreams begin to mend.
As night falls soft, they drift away,
Embraced by the dawn of a new day.

Each wish a star, a flickering flame,
In the silence, they call your name.
When moments meet the fading light,
They dance in the silence of the night.

As dreams wane down like autumn's leaves,
The heart collects what hope believes.
In quietude, a peace takes hold,
The stories whispered, soft yet bold.

Yet even as the visions fade,
In stillness, new dreams are made.
For night may steal what day has spun,
But hope will rise with every sun.

So let them fade, let silence reign,
For in the quiet, we love again.
From dreams, we learn what it means to be,
In the soft embrace of memory.

The Pausing Breath of Ancient Paths

On ancient paths where echoes lay,
The earth remembers every sway.
Each footfall marked in dust and stone,
A melody, a world unknown.

The trees stand tall, their secrets kept,
Guardians of dreams and promises swept.
With every step, we pause to hear,
The whispered tales from those held dear.

In sunlight's glow, the shadows blend,
As time weaves on, we must contend.
With every breath, the past awakes,
In every pause, a journey takes.

So walk with care, respect the stride,
For in each path, the stories bide.
In breaths that linger, lessons dwell,
Ancient paths hold magic's spell.

In every pause, in silence deep,
The roots of history we shall keep.
For time reveals what hearts ignore,
In pauses taken, we find much more.

9 781805 651154